ALSO BY DIANE WAKOSKI

Coins & Coffins (1962)
Four Young Lady Poets (1962)
Discrepancies and Apparitions (1966)
The George Washington Poems (1967)
Greed: Parts 1 & 2 (1968)
The Diamond Merchant (1968)
Inside the Blood Factory (1968)
Thanking My Mother for Piano Lessons (1969)
The Lament of the Lady Bank Dick (1969)
Greed: Parts 3 & 4 (1969)
The Moon Has a Complicated Geography (1969)
Black Dream Ditty (1970)
The Magellanic Clouds (1970)
Greed: Parts 5-7 (1971)
On Barbara's Shore (1971)
The Motorcycle Betrayal Poems (1971)
Form Is an Extension of Content (1972)
Smudging (1972)
The Pumpkin Pie (1972)
Greed: Parts 8, 9 & 11 (1973)
Dancing on the Grave of a Son of a Bitch (1973)
Looking for the King of Spain (1974)
Trilogy: Coins & Coffins, Discrepancies and Apparitions,
      The George Washington Poems (1974)
The Fable of the Lion and the Unicorn (1975)
Creating a Personal Mythology (1975)
The Wandering Tattler (1975)
Virtuoso Literature for Two and Four Hands (1975)
Variations on a Theme (1976)
Waiting for the King of Spain (1976)
Pachelbel's Canon (1978)
The Man Who Shook Hands (1978)
Trophies (1979)
Cap of Darkness (1980)
The Magician's Feastletters (1982)
The Collected Greed, Parts 1-13 (1984)

Diane Wakoski

The Rings
of
Saturn

Black Sparrow Press
Santa Rosa · 1986

LIBRARY OF CONGRESS CATALOGING-IN-PUBLICATION DATA

Wakoski, Diane.
    The rings of Saturn.

    Poems.
    I. Title.
PS3573.A42R56 1986   811'.54   86-9539
ISBN 0-87685-675-X
ISBN 0-87685-676-8 (signed)
ISBN 0-87685-674-1 (pbk.)

Contents

The Rings of Saturn

Mrs. Van Blair's Aviary

A whole room for birds.
What extravagance, how wonderful, I thought,
for my mother and sister and I
lived in a 3-room shack, in the same orange grove that
    bordered
the Van Blair's big sprawling house.
She mashed up hard-
boiled eggs to feed the canaries, and I thought it was like
cannibalism, their eating eggs, though they were
chicken eggs, not the little nuggets
the canaries laid.
She had goats that my mother milked
when the Van Blairs went
on vacation, and there was a croquet set
on the lawn that I loved
to be invited to play with. Mrs. Van Blair was fat
(I saw her naked once/ it was quite ugly),
always looked tired,
gave piano lessons,
and had big-boned children who looked
like camp counselors.
I don't know what she
and my poor, bookkeeping mother
had in common. My mother's husband
had left her, and Mrs. Van Blair's was a judge.
Maybe neither one had sex,
or both loved flowers?
Maybe neither could accept getting old
or both were amazed at how fast life passed them
by?
Maybe they both had headaches,
or were constipated? Whatever it was,
it didn't show. On the
surface one seemed like a woman of property,

the other, a poor working woman.
But they both loved to stand outside the glass
of the aviary and watch the 30 or so canaries
singing, chattering, fluttering about. Neither
minded the mess or the trouble. Both said
they could sit or stand
and watch the birds all day.

The Woman Who Wears Grey

Soft as a pigeon, a mourning dove,
her hands are partridges
that lie in her lap, as a nest. Her wedding dress
was grey silk, soft as water,
like an opal with little fires burning in it.

Eleven days after the wedding
the groom, her husband, killed himself
by hanging. She walked in
to find him grotesquely dead and wondered —
her anger, her bewilderment, her hurt;
why did he go through the wedding ceremony? Only
to take this violent leave? Was it
to punish her? Why did he hate her? How could
anyone hate that much?

The moon is a place of dead craters, made perhaps
by falling cosmic debris, unbuffeted by the moon's
low field of gravity. She wears her grey wedding dress,
as soft as water, to the funeral
to remind everyone
that nothing has changed in her life. The man she
married two weeks ago must have written the suicide note
even before he took his vows, and she was dressed as
the mourning dove,
even from the beginning;
but how will we know
and how can we stop thinking without our eyes turning
into roses, whose soft petals fall off in the corridors.

It does not help to know.
One day I hold the moon, full as a pigeon breast, in my
     hand,
the next, it is empty and crackling like paper.

Removed from Natural Habitat

The feathers are thick and look sculptured,
as if they are curved, like cherries, not flat or straight.
And they grow down over the claws,
like little bedroom slippers, of fur, becoming lacy
at the ground. Also, curved
over their bills, the feathers disguise the raptor's beak,
making it protrude only like a pursed mouth
below eyes like golden coins. Part of their beauty is
in their stillness, the unblinking eyes like money that is
    hoarded,
the head cocked a little, the body stationary, and seemingly
unjointed.

White as new field mushrooms,
are the males; one stands there,
plump and unblemished, making me wonder what he sees, if
    anything.
The females are barred, wearing their thick
horizontal stripes as if the shadow of a prison window
had fallen on their bodies. They too
stand motionless for hours, the fringed white slippers
over their claws moving a little with the afternoon
breeze.

I too stood motionless for a long time
one afternoon, watching them,
though if my image was on the retina of even one snowy
    owl,
it could not have given any bird
the solace I found that day,
looking at these three creatures, placid, though totally
    removed
from their natural habitat.

A Snowy Winter in East Lansing

We feed the birds
leaving mixed corn and millet and sunflower seeds
in a big pole feeder,
thistle seed in two small tubes,
and pure sunflower kernels in a domed plastic globe,
but only the sparrows come, hundreds of them,
an occasional chickadee,
and one lonesome pair of finches.

After two years,
we no longer expect other birds, though
we long for flashing cardinals, noisy
blue jays, purple finches, towhees, downy
and hairy woodpeckers.

But in this part of the midwest,
the land is flat and monotonous,
there are no good restaurants,
and even our friends seem to leach out
each year, or become flattened
by the terrain. So,
                    I've stopped
believing that even the birdfeeders
could yield surprise
or drama,
or colour,
for that matter;
I like the life,
the sense that we've done all we can.
And the English sparrows,
sitting like little candles in the big
yew bushes, heaped with fluffy snow —
they have their beauty too,
if looked at,
with certain eyes.

What Would Tennessee Williams Have Said

Is there drama in everyday life?
I wonder
as I boil the water for my
morning tea.
The tea has stained
the white porcelain parts of the pot so that they look
like the feathers of a sparrow. I scrub,
but the crazed surface
inside
bares its old horse teeth at me,
impossible with stain.

The half dozen evening grosbeaks
flying up in yellow and black flurry,
as if someone has torn the business pages
out of the phone directory and thrown
them up in the air,
flying from the asphalt pavement
of the woodsy road we were driving,
the surprise of their beauty,
their unfamiliarity, like seeing the hundreds
of small purple wild iris
along the same road, for the first time.
Also startling.
Exciting.
But were those moments
dramatic?
Or the most dramatic events
that happen in my daily life? What
would Tennessee Williams have said,
I wonder, about the last poetry program
I was asked to give?
When the director wanted me to wear
a cape and

14

invited me to a dinner party in his kitchen
where we ate with his senile mother, victim of Alzheimer's
    disease.
        No drinks were offered but
        herb tea. He
        was making cheddar cheese soup
        out of a plastic bottle of something processed
        and his mother would say things like,
        "I'm hungry. I want some bingbang now,"
        and
        "I saw her coming out of the refrigerator
        with a nogger and she birded it,"
        and, flaring up with anger,
        "You'd better give me some more to eat or I'll cruise."
        The aging house they lived in was stacked with
                        newspapers, and
        he ironed his
        trousers while we waited for the nurse
        to come and stay with his mother.
        When we got to the theater
        there were only six
        people
        in the audience. I wore the cape
        for a while,
        but it jingled and was hot. It was a beautiful
        garment, a sculpture
        really, but not made
        for giving poetry readings.

        The director told me at length how
        he cares for his senile mother,
        who is incontinent and who eats
        everything she finds, like a baby. We saw
        this at dinner, as she kept chewing
        parts of her paper napkin.
        How can you not admire

a man who will stay at home
and care for a senile mother; yet
how can you not hate him
for inviting you to dinner, as celebration for a
        performance/
you are nervous, in a strange place, not knowing who
        will be there/
with his senile mother,
eating in the kitchen, while he irons his trousers,
with neither alcohol, caffeine or festive food to
alleviate the tension. A pretense
that we are not strangers, or have a friendship
that does not exist?

Where is the drama
or poetry?
I see only
humiliation,
and my own sense of meanness
that the whole night angered me
and reduced me to these petty
observations.
What *would* Tennessee Williams have said
about that evening?
That you can turn anything trivial
into art? What do *I* say
about it?
That I was humiliated,
made aware of the foolishness and triviality
of my own life.
That for the past two months
I have felt over and over
how petty and mean it is
to resent being asked to dinner in a kitchen with a senile
        stranger.

16

Yet, I see her,
again and again,
in her blue cotton shirtwaist dress,
eating her paper napkin,
speaking like a mad child,
and her son, who wiped off our plates, as well as hers, with
     the
pink sponge between soup and salad,
scrubbing down his mother's dress after the meal
with the same sponge, pink
on her baby blue dress.
Robert and I escaped finally to the yard,
he smoking,
I wondering
what vision of myself,
the future,
this event was supposed to make me take
away?
Wondering what
Tennessee Williams would have done,
or if some things really are
too petty or mean
or cruel
for art. Whereas life
absorbs everything?

Some animals, like foxes,
kill the old when they are no longer cunning enough
to survive alone.

Clint's Bottle of 1977 Châteauneuf du Pape

Robert bought a finch feeder &
immediately attracted
two finches.
I played my computer blackjack game
all day.
There was sun on
the snow.
Clint came at 7 wearing his
outrageous t-shirt,

We had New England Boiled Dinner
and drank
the CNdP.

The Fear of Fat Children

upon the return of a much food-
stained copy of Bukowski's
Dangling in the Tournefortia,
by a fat student

Age has blown me up like the wind spirit
of a Chinese river, whose
belly
hangs out over stylized waves, looking like the scales
of a carp. Ancient fish
with bevelled fins swim up
from the past for crumbs carried in a greasy paper. That
must have been what was lying next to the book
you borrowed,
John, fat boy, with monster-face,
who sweats and smells like dirty socks
in our hot spring afternoon classroom. But it is age,
the approach of death, which has treated my body thus,
not birth, life, youth.
How these surfaces punish us,
yet when I ask myself which punishes more —
                    surface or interior —
I know
        I know
                    Can't
be satisfied.

Legally, we've just investigated Marilyn Monroe's death for
        signs
of murder, because we can't
just can't, believe she, with the luscious surface,
a melon, a lichee nut,
could have reason to kill herself.

And, it is foolish of me to worry so
about your sweaty fat body, your fleshy bat-nose
flattened across your face, your smelly hands
which cannot allow you
to read a book without its looking as if you fried bacon
over it. Yet "fat"
has always been coupled with
"old" in my vocabulary.
And to me has always been a sign of
defeat.

                    I am afraid
of fat children,
of flesh in the young,
for it seems to be what death and the grave
are all about.
I am fat from drinking California cabernets,
eating chèvres, and crisp breads,
from pâtés and pasta genovese, cognac, butter,
vichyssoise, a summer of
tomatoes, an autumn of squash,
whereas you told me you ate packaged macaroni
dinners, and I am sure day-old doughnuts
and potato chips accompany every
page
you turn.

John, I wanted to give you
the Bukowski book
that summer day you returned it, greasy and limp,
but one look told me I couldn't.
There was my fear too,
of your young fatness,
and death.
I looked out the door
and did not see you,

but a mirror
of what I fear.
                    It is not
fat children,
but my own death, age.

The fat of wasted life.

The Girls

for Margaret Atwood & Cathy Davidson

I never understood the girls
who had the sweaters
and the latest hairdos copied out of magazines
and who were not afraid of snakes.
They were the thin-hipped ones who looked good
in straight skirts, like exclamation points
behind phrases like "Wow," and "Gee Whiz."

I envied their lemon-scented hands
raised to answer almost as many questions
as I, the ugly duckling class brain, did,
with my fat ankles,
and ass as soft as a sofa pillow.
Valerie Twadell who was Miss La Habra
at our August Corn Festival
chased me with worms.

Cathy, with her Zelda-ish bob,
and slimness that even her sorority girl students envy
tells of a snake they ritually put in the 8th grade teacher's
        desk;
and now you, Peggy, as I heard someone nice
call you, slender and chic as Jane Fonda,
tell of your own simple connection with snakes,
wearing them as electric tight bracelets,
wound on a willow wrist,
the delight you took in scaring others,
even men, or women like me,
who would have died had we found even a harmless little
        black
fellow
curled in the grass.

I have never been
one of the girls:
smart without being labelled with derogatory titles like
                    "the encyclopedia"
                    "the brain,"
graceful without watching calories,
followed by men who adored me even when I turned them
        away,
slow-voiced,
quiet,
with ankles like colts,
and at complete ease with snakes.
I have never been
one of the girls.
At 47, I still envy your cool acceptance
of all these gifts.
                    Some part of me
was denied
what all women have,
or are supposed to have, an ease
with the fatly coiled Python whose skin
is like milky underwear,
the thread-like green mamba who slips past
your fingers like mountain water,
the cobra who sits on the family radio
in Sri Lanka,
the cottonmouth who swims next to you all night
in muddy fertile loving water,
or the magic necklace Denise imagines
around her throat.

Men see me as the Medusa,
with vipers hissing around my hair.
How ironic/ I have always been so afraid
of snakes that when I was six

I couldn't turn to the S N A K E page
in my Golden Encyclopedia.

I have never been one of the girls,
comfortable wearing a blacksnake as a belt.
Had I been Lawrence,
near his well in Sicily,
I would have turned and run. He knew
snakes were
the Lords of Life,
but I know you pretty girl women,
who handle them like hula hoops,
or jump ropes,
or pet kittens,
are the real Gods, and your ease with snakes
is proof.
In your presence I am neither man
nor woman. I am simply the one
afraid of snakes; who knows
that in this life
it is the one thing
not allowed.

Aging in Dubrovnik

Some grow grizzled
while others bloat into their mothers.
None of us can ever feel
in touch
with the distorted image.
        In the cafe,
        the 40-year-old mother
        stroking her Adriatic tan,
        a body still lean,
        now so smooth with sun,
        she is completely absorbed
        in the fire which glows out of her
        arms, her neck;
        in touch,
        to herself,
        she is young,
        her husband, a quiet, slim
        dignified man, like a well-behaved
        weimaraner, greying to silver
Then arrives teen-age daughter and friend.
Hair bleached golden by the sun,
sparkling coral finger-tips, show-girl legs,
each face masked for the night
with Elizabeth Taylor eyelashes.
Every movement is fresh.
Oh, mother, look inward now
to stroke your own silky arms,
for golden daughter will
without even knowing why,
steal father away;
all men will look at her
until you are neuter.
        A man
who says he prefers 40-year-olds

to 20-year women
is lying.
Oh, mothers, mothers, stroke your arms,
look inward,
to where you are still young
and more beautiful than
your daughters.

The Lady Who Drove Me to the Airport

Big Robert stands dusky, holding
the silver King Salmon,
20 pounds, with a wide-open fish mouth,
which blessedly, never talked.

The canyon of morning glory vines
spreads below a window where I stand
and the purple flowers also open
flower lips, which thrill the air
with their silence.

Finally, at home, I turn on air
conditioner, electric typewriter, even
the ignition of my auto,
and their noise is steady, quiet.
How I hate the human voice
after being trapped on the Long Island Expressway
for nearly three hours with that woman's steady
chatter.

Her growing hysteria with night driving,
the freeway, her inability to follow directions.

I leapt like a spawning fish
trying to return home.
She tried to drive me.
Madness is catching.

*   *   *

Why do you suppose anyone
would want to tell you
her ex-husband used to masturbate
in front of the colour television?

Or that after being married to her for 25 years
he just wanted to live alone?

Stupidity?
Guilt?

Poor man. I started the afternoon
sympathizing with the pathos
of a lonely aging woman
and ended the evening wondering why
the masturbating husband
hadn't murdered her?
Or left 20 years before?

Was she ever young and quiet?
Was her mouth ever like a fresh fig?
Full, sticky,
softly quiet?

The lady who drove me to the airport
this week
lies coiled in my trunk
like a rattlesnake,
waiting to spring at me. She is
there
to remind me of evil,
a pathetic broken housewife
who can't change lanes on a freeway,
who doesn't know how to use a rearview mirror,
who talks incessantly like a broken tape in a space ship,
saying over and over,
"Input. I need input. Input. I need input."

I flee from her car when she finally locates
the airport,
my gills heaving.

Why did I make this journey?
To hold,
to embrace,
warm, silent self;
a tired fish spawning in old waters?

The chilly steelhead fear
that every woman's failure
is my own?

Stones

Cast a white grid
still as oil.
The reflecting water
shrugs its undulating shoulders,
the stones' light, a shawl
over this sleeping woman's torso.

Lovćen *

Climbing the stairs
                up
                up
Susan says we are going to heaven.

At grandmother's house
the long stairs
lead to her chair
where she sits rocking, holding
a bucket of cherries,
Bings,
from the Willamette Valley orchard.
She is singing in German,
crocheting the edges of pillow slips
smooth under our sleepy heads.
                Down,
                down,
                they are coming
                behind me.
The ghosts of every mistaken moment
in my life.
            On this September mountainside
where everyone is surer of
his footing than I,
what a luxury it is
to sit here,
neither to climb up,
nor down.

Oh, mother, you have made me so
fearful

---

*Lovćen refers to a monument in Montenegro, a remarkable tomb at
the top of a mountain. The tomb is dedicated to poet, Njegosh.

I cannot even climb the stairs
                    to my grandmother
and her room full of cherries,
the blossoms spill out of this
tomb.

I would climb these stairs,
but I cannot;
they stretch like the tongue of a liar
farther than truth or history.
The blossoms cover my feet.
Cherries, cherries in my mouth.
I am the wood of the cherry tree.
I cannot go up or down,
the truth is in me.
                    Grandmother rocks
at the top of the stairs
while someone sharpens George Washington's hatchet,
its blade lying shiny
near my blossoming feet.

Grandmother waits with her
bucket of Bings
at the top of the stairs.

Sveti Stefan*

for David and Annette

Imagine every house
with an arbor of grapevines
and on each lattice hang
bunches of purpling grapes.
6 a.m.
The waiter is spreading white cloths
on the breakfast tables,
white as the foam breaking on the rocks.
Here at the foot of the mountains
in Montenegro,
                    Crna Gora,
someone is burning the toast,
and I think of our California
Malibu coast;
                    old friends,
the Adriatic
looks like
such a quiet sea.

---

*Sveti Stefan is a seaside resort town on the Montenegro coast.

Braised Leeks & Framboise

for Annette Smith

The ocean
this morning
has tossed someone's garbage
over its surface,
half oranges
that make my mouth pucker for
fresh juice,
lettuce leaves
looking fragile, decorative, like scarves
for the white curling locks
of old water.
It is not hard
to think of women
coming up out of the dense green,
fully formed but not
of flesh, of some tissue, floating
goddess-like
and pale.

For breakfast
one morning
you served fresh leeks, slender
as fingers, from a sea goddess,
braised, with butter, delicate
from the Altadena garden.

It was at your house
that I first drank
that clear heady liquor,
framboise,
an eau de vie, promising
that fruit did not have to be

fresh-cheeked, fat or stupid,
that it could read Proust,
or learn differential
equations.
The Saturnian taste
of old raspberries, and the moon's
clear-fingered insistence
of leek. These two intangible things
I owe you,
along with — what? or
is there more?

The image of an onion, its sweet blanket layers.
The pebbled surface
of a raspberry.

For Clint in East Lansing While I Am Sitting on the
    Adriatic Coast

I've bought figs every day
almost.
And looking at the sea in the morning
is better than sitting in our patio
at home.
But it is the ocean I love,
not other languages, or cultures.

Michigan is not the only place
where there's no
native cuisine/ what we cannot
forget
is how civilization and imagination
allows someone to take what is available —
                the salmon,
                or the cherries,
                the asparagus,
                or millet,
                or squid,
                or milk,
                a certain kind of grape,
                rosemary growing wild,
and turn it into
a remarkable food.

And that without a real sense
of possibility,
even an imaginative dish
like pizza
can turn into tasteless cardboard
with bad tomato paste and dull cheese
as it is in hundreds of restaurants
in East Lansing.

Never thought I'd get tired of
grilled meat,
but after three weeks here in Yugoslavia
I did. It is variety we need some-
times. A view of the ocean,
though;
perhaps if I had that daily,
I should never
want change or care so much
about the imaginative use
of natural ingredients.

Grain

The midwest is a king-size package
of cereal.
Husks of wheat rustling into a bowl
like dry leaves in autumn,
the sound of field mice playing in the mushrooming dark
of an empty kitchen.
                              And driving
to work in the seed of a car
in winter, snow crusting with its sugary lid
the bowl of warm meal, Michigan earth,
also home of asparagus and the square tomato, I see
the sun swathed in a flannel of snow,
a dim orange glow in the morning's sky
behind a bare-limbed tree.
                              PARIS,
I think,
                              at sunset,
but I was only once
in Paris,
a New Year's Eve, arriving at the Gare du Nord
from Salzburg, in Alpine snow,
the raw fingers of the waiter shucking oysters for us
in a cafe,
the traditional champagne/ I don't
remember
any sunsets,
but that scene, those ice-water reddened hands,
red as any California sunset,
the end of my marriage to a man who could not love
        women/ or was it
only
ME?
Winter comes every year, crusting over the stubbed grain
        fields,

here in the midwest
where, driving to work in the snow,
I sometimes think I am in
the city of Paris.
                    In summer
I look out my back windows into the oak trees
and pretend that beyond
the back fence
is the Pacific Ocean.
                    Rustling leaves
make me
think I hear it. If there is so much beauty
in longing, surely it is hope then
that makes us happy,
not satisfaction.
My memory of Paris is filled with pain.
When I lived on the Pacific Ocean
also
(pain).
The object itself does not hold beauty;
nor the thought of it;
but the hope of what it might be.
A grain of wheat,
black earth,
the sun, like thick ice-water reddened hands
opening the New Year's Eve oysters.

Crocus

On the oak table
in my office
they flaunt their stamens.
Saffron tongues
in dying purple.
Their rags
in my bedroom
where I had flocked them
20 or 30 purple punching bags
when they first bloomed,
smooth as eggplant,
shiny, globed, and bulging
with spring.

They are on the lawn now,
early April,
close to the ground,
blue and white eyes looking up
out of the earth, gold flecked
pupils, the saffron lesson
makes me want to pick them,
but I leave them.
                    Perhaps they
will teach me
earthly truths. Ones I need to know.
How to be admired,
not trampled.

How to come back
each spring,
relentlessly beautiful,
in the same place.

The Handicapped at Risen Hotel

At first,
the boy seemed to be counting
in his head,
some addition the room clerk
has just presented him with.
But later, we see him on the terrace
in the cafe,
moving his head spasmodically the same way,
a clock's mechanism which infinitely
repeats.
He is joined at the table by a man whose
mouth is sideways
on his face,
one whose hands seem
to mistake themselves
for pliers,
and a girl whose ankles are limbs of white birch,
unbending even though they are attached to a foot.

Cappuccino,
Espresso,
the sun sparkling like cognac on the sea,
we are whole
on the outside,
but recognize our interiors
with silence and some horror
in this table of visitors
from the Risen Home/
for the Handicapped.

The Ukranian Rose

Beefy Anna,
our super on East Fifth St.,
who loved her son, the gambler,
who wore an angel babushka
and carried the garbage cans out each week,
stood gossiping in her small American vocabulary
about the tenants who didn't pay their rents,
the one whose dog chewed up the kitchen linoleum and
    Eddie
the book maker who was shot in the Tip Top Bar
across the street.

She had human life
and, I think, little else. I'm sure even
in the Ukraine as a child she was heavy
as grain threshing equipment
and not clever. No star in the kitchen,
or anywhere else.
How did she marry, immigrate to New York,
have a baby, learn to speak even her
rudimentary English? What
biology carried her forward into a life
I cannot imagine
wanting to live? What rose did she see
unfolding each day,
petal by petal, lush and engulfing even the garbage cans
of Fifth St.? Rose, rose, rose,
c'est la vie?

Good Water

the cup holds
a ball,
the ball becomes
a skull,
the skull breaks
into matchsticks,
the matchsticks congeal
into gold,
the gold powders
into the dust on a moth's wing,
the moth wing expands
and is a blanket of silk,
the blanket of silk covers a foot,
the foot belongs to someone who
never cuts his toenails,
the long sharp toenails,
like trowels, repel dirt, they
dig into the soil/ a man
becomes a garden tool,
the garden tool hangs
in the garage,
the garage is closed for the winter,
winter is full of snow,
the snow melts into water,
the water is in the cup.

The Man with the Shoe Button Eyes

for David Bottoms

You remind me
of train stations,
of the order of polished shoes,
of mornings in hotels
when a comfortable breakfast waits
in the dining room.

Neat hands
sweep the world into your own sense
of order. Your smooth hair
could be
artificial, a beautifully made
doll's.

I would trust you
to arrange a timetable for me, and to
smoke your cigar
where it wouldn't stink up a room. You might be
the perfect father,
silent, smelling of a discreet
aftershave, always
with quarters in your pockets,
none of those joking remarks about sex
that so embarrass children, or frighten them.

You are younger than I,
but seem
so solid. A pocket watch;
an honest salesman
in a world of hustlers.
An uncle
I would have liked to have.

Tight

this dark room
with one window full of morning sun
filtered through
a curtain

the fireplace
immense
as long as an ox

where would
a Brooklyn boy
see ox-herders
or why
write about them/ he
feared leprosy
as a child
more than anything
fingers and toes
dropping off
but when
I called for him
in the parking lot, he
wd not speak.
He wanted to lead,
not to follow
but even the girls he chose
were plunging down
under the earth, he had to follow
just to be part of any story/ hero follows
to rescue

but the break in the voice
indicates
sorrow.

It is not love leading anyone
to hell, but the desire
to go down and bury oneself
in the source
of Spring.

Light

I live for books
and light to read them in.
                              Waterlilies
reaching up
from the depths of the pond
algae dark,
the frog loves a jell of
blue-green water,
                              the bud
scales
a rope of stem,
then floats in sunshine. Like soap
in the morning bath.
This book I read
floats in my hand like a waterlily
coming out of the nutrient waters
of thought
and light shines on us both,
the morning's breviary.

Walking in the Herb Garden with Barbara Drake

Summer,
your husband shooting pistols
in the back fields, the half-dingo dog
calmer, now that you are here,
but the damp concrete-floored house
in Okemos is only a husk,
a carapace you've slit, your new
wet body glistening with possibilities.

Yesterday,
I didn't call
though I knew you'd be loading
the rental truck, and might even slip away
from Michigan, beginning your Westward
journey this morning while I slept.
I didn't call
because I sensed the moving,
loading all your antique American
plain-wood cabinets, pie safes,
and tables, along with cartons of books,
unlike most moving,
where we enjoin every friend we can
to help, was a private severance.
Would Moss, your eldest son, help you,
or be off, writing science fiction?
Would Bud, pistol-packing handsome
hot-rod husband, Bud, lay down
his anger for a moment,
unloaded, a Smith & Wesson,
a Browning, a Colt, on the table
and help you move away from him
to another city where at last you've found
a decent job, one that won't burn
you out before you write all

your best poems; or would he explode
with the volcanic feelings your refusal of his life has mixed?

Morning,
summer now,
earlier than when we walked in the campus herb garden
last week, steaming in the near-noon air,
looking at injurious plants, such as
nightshade and monkshood, oleander
and castor bean.
Wandering, like curious women, we are
among names as well as plants:
snow-on-the-mountain,
rape,
choke cherry,
matrimony vine,
staggerweed.
And I wonder how it is
that two people can live together twenty years
and still know so little
about each other,
be so helpless at providing
satisfaction or even
comfort, at preventing
unparallel growth and change. How is
it that, all these years, he
could not see that by doing nothing
his job got better and better,
while you knocked yourself out
term after term and yours got worse and worse?
How could a man *not*
understand that a job is one thing
you do change
your life for?   Easy answer:
because it's what a man
changes his life for,
not a woman.

But you, in your quiet way,
making do with imperfect prisms,
and your willingness to lend your sanity
to crazy ladies,
told him over and over,
the heart is a muscle, not a valentine;
it gets stronger and stronger with use.
And when he finally would not
understand
that you lived for family and poetry,
that you hated change
but that you hated your job more,
when he finally would not
understand this
love
at the Egyptian Theater
was not just exotic childishness
but womanly truth,
he still refused to accept,
and decided you were running away
to a lover.

But, your lover is a school which will
treat you with respect,
honor your talents; a city where
your daughter, who says she won't ever
come back to Michigan, can get
a real education; a landscape
with a coast, an ocean, and a real
volcano; a state with a history
of personal independence and
self-help politics.   How could you
not love these things, and yes,
they love you too?

Maybe I stayed away yesterday
also
because I am not sure
how I
would behave
in equal circumstances. I have never
been a graceful loser,
when a husband or lover was leaving me; I too,
like Bud,
always thought
he was leaving
for a woman, not for Vermont or Washington, D.C.
or because life with me had become the wrong pattern, one
he didn't want any
longer.
How we are all
always repeating history.

Today,
I sip this tea
in Michigan's August summer morning,
fat with tomatoes, the fragrance
of basil growing on my roof, one long
pod of wisteria hanging like a small
green necktie over the terrace. I stay here for what I have,
what this state gives me.

Today,
you drove away
in a rented truck, to I-80,
not with Paradise and Moriarty but
Moss and Monica, your
teenage children. Why
would you ever come
back to this place where ladies
hang themselves with belts

in their basements,
a state that boasts
the murder capital,
and the highest unemployment rate?

If only Bud had said,
    "O love,
      where are you
    leading
      me now?"
               or
    "And so, I missed my chance with one of the lords
    Of life.
    And I have something to expiate;
    A pettiness."
instead of,
    "I thought hard for us all — my only swerving —
    then pushed her over the edge into the river."

But we don't necessarily live
the poetry we write, or love.
How
I miss you in this pure American midwestern place, Barbara,
walking among the rue and silver sage.

Cannon Beach

One week of early morning sunshine, like a perfect rose
    frozen into an ice cube,
made us so grateful, we then loved the mist
which rolled in and blanketed us for days.
When the sun shone, we walked
the beach at dawn
while most people slept, but on the foggy mornings,
we slept too, not even hearing the horns
sounding from the rocks. Two thousand miles away,
I can only pretend to see the Pacific Ocean
no matter how early I rise.
The mist that steams up from this autumn ground
over pumpkins, the dried dinner-plate sun flowers
with bowed heads, the final red tomatoes on the browning
vines, a different beauty. It is as if everyone
in Cannon Beach is sleeping
while I'm awake, everyone, everywhere,
different from this landscape, sleeping,
only I awake, not knowing the images in each head;
as we all sleep through others' lives.

Only a few even try to imagine
what others simultaneously perceive,
and then know its futility. An act of faith
lets me believe the Pacific Ocean's still there, since I now
can't see it. That the sun exists,
though the fog entirely covers it today. That in my
sleep, I do not lose all identity, or in death
pass beyond what I now know I am.

Why My Mother Likes Liberace

(Liberace has many large diamond rings and
impressively wears a great number of them
even when he plays very difficult music)

The diamond grand,
its lid upraised,
the diamond butterfly,
the diamonds of South African mines,
clasping his fingers,
one for every tour, one ring for
his fortieth anniversary
in show business, all sitting
as if they were in howdahs, above his
fingers,
which continue to move as if
utterly
unencumbered. Not elephants but manatees
swimming in the Crystal River,
glissandos,
arpeggios, weaving hands, moving
like dragonflies
though they resemble hod-carriers
more, with the diamond-loads,
an effort of masonry.

What does it mean
never to get tired
of playing jingle bells or Chopin,
to have a chandelier
in your greenhouse,
or piano keyboard painted on the door
of one of your limousines,
to love men,
to wear silly shirts,

to have millions of pathetic old women
in love with you
    my mother:
                yr only rival with her —
Lawrence Welk.

Why am I, the girl who gave up
the piano
to make meaning out of her life,
who never watches television,
does not own a tv set,
watching with such seriousness
this talk show
with Liberace telling about
each diamond ring he wears?
Why
thinking with admiration
of his skill, equal to most
great pianists?
              Why
am I wishing
for as much shape and purpose
from any such burden of diamonds
and tinkling keys?

Why do so many of us admire,
long for,
men who only love other men?

Do we need betrayers
and deniers
to reinforce our own failures?
Or are we searching for
some final answer,
beyond the greater measure,
beyond sex,
beyond our own mortality?

On the Boardwalk in Atlantic City

Early September,
and the day still a nymph of a day,
the ocean a rippled silk handkerchief,
the sandy flat beach
cool, without bodies yet packing their density
into its planes,
empty cabana tents, striped gold and white for recognition,
the inevitable middle-aged man
with a metal-detector gliding his wand over
the beach.

We hug our paper cups of hot coffee and tea
sit on the cement benches
of a shaded pavilion
and survey the others out here at 9:30 a.m.

We are waiting for the casino at Caesar's Palace
to open its doors, 10 a.m.
Waiting to grab one of the few nickel slot machines
to play for 3 or 4 hours before patience
and $20 run out. We wish
we were in The West,
Las Vegas,
but instead we are in this old crumbling
place, sleeping at The Flamingo Motel.
Oh, what are we doing to change the world?
Now is the time to go West.
I want to be headed
for Liberace's house on the desert,
the greenhouse with
the chandelier,
the station wagon with an octave of piano keys
painted along its side.
The desert and

atom bombs, some
sense of myself
in territory I recognize.

Some Pumpkins

lie
on our patio brick

Robert says
now
I can read
each autumn morning
by pumpkin light.

Seeing Robert in the Crystal Ball

He's in the corner,
a figure like a crow
with one long shoe, like a tree reaching over
water.
An upsidedown lighted lamp
floats on the other side of the room,
like a cow grazing in a field.
There are three other people
in this room,
but none in the ball. Only crow-Robert,
on his cottonwood shoe, with his
lighted-cow,
that once was a room.

The Man Who Slurps His Drink

Education
for the football player
who's smart as an eagle
but a big messy bird, whose stinking nest
you'd never want to visit,
convinces me
that not everything can be learned.

Is it possible,

I ask myself,
for a man to be sensitive to words
when he slurps his drink? Can what
comes out
of the mouth have fineness
when it goes in so offensively?
Perhaps I need more anthropology
to give me wisdom/perspective?

I know the Chinese are trained
to belch and slurp
to show satisfaction over a good meal.

Did this man's

Chicago slum life
teach him to slurp his drink
in my house
to show appreciation?

Am I a

hopeless prig,
or is it just hard for me to dismiss
language I don't believe,
unless some bodily condition seems
to reinforce
my view.

What would you think
if you heard someone

slurping
a bloody mary
in your
living room?
      Would you really expect him
to be a poet?

Queen of Wands

One week
these flowering pear
quince
cherry
beautiful girls on their wooden
swings
move in the air/Spring a
season Southern Californians
never feel.
                    Why
I wonder
does the old poet
want to believe that Williams
was an out-of-control satyr,
or that his wife deeply
unhappy in her marriage, longed for divorce?
Are we all obsessed with ourselves to the extent that we
        cannot   *
see others?
                    This weekly orange truck
is filling with refuse.
We paint it orange, symbolic of fire,
transformation.
I am the chameleon in the heart of that fire,
glowing red, incandescent,
now a heart, now a smiling face, now
the remainder of a hand
or the beginning of one/ change me from
this garbage
into something pure. Oh, change me.

The Leaf on the Outdoor Table

in September
is half green, half
brown. It
lies
in a perfect circle
of water
formed by the plastic surface which looking
smooth,
has slightly buckled
into
concavity. The wood of the
patio deck
is weathered gray. Two
pumpkins glow
against it. My asparagus fern which comes out
of the small light room upstairs
each summer to
drink in Michigan's humidity
is competing now, for another week,
before returning to its
inner place
with the yew whose berries
are reddening faster. Could
there be a way to bring
the petunias climbing their stone pots
indoors too? No,
they must be abandoned to the season. Why? Too
lazy? No space?
An acceptance of summer flowers
being left to
the summer? Why bring
anything in then? Live
with the natural?
                    Not unless

it is the most beautiful.
I reject nature firmly
when it does not suit me.

Memory

There are days when
it closes
like a book you have finished;
when you have been left with nothing
to say.

But today
it unrolls, like a carpet,
woven by many hands, though finally
dated
in arabic
and signed by only one,
red wool practically
unfaded
from lying in the mosque so many years,
a darkened place.

This sea is so beautiful,
no one needs religion here; the sun
would fade away any woven fabric,
the salt erode it,
but the small waves break against
each rock with a spume
like dolphin breath,
it wets the rock as a memory,
leaving a darkened patch which
in the bright hours
of the morning will dry and disappear.

Is it possible that many books are
so written?
With stories that must be read
at once,
or not at all?

When You Want to Change Your Life Study the Birds

two jays
like knives being honed, are
talking
to each other this morning. Now one, at least
a block away, rasps his voice edge
along the steel, over and over,
a punctuating chickadee (dee, dee, dee)
a few acorns falling with their plastic rattle

September morning in Michigan.

Smoke

Smoke from chimneys
in winter
is the breath
of the house. Makes you wonder
as you see people on
the street, and their breath billowing out
of mouths as clouds
if there is not also some fire of snapping flames
consuming logs of ash and cedar, oak,
maple, birch. Right in
the belly,
an orange-flamed fire,
burning and pushing
those steamy clumps of language
into the air.

George Washington's Autumn

Could he have seen flashes
of the boardwalk at Atlantic City,
September 1983,
the beach like a beautiful well-formed mouth,
not smiling but solemnly inviting
one into the ocean
which is black and forever, no thought of
ships or sailboats, no swimmers alive,
a place where the dead join
the other waste of civilization?

These mornings when it is cool and
the orange umbrellas are
not yet up,
the sand white, shaded with charcoal,
your face and mine,
familiar behind hot paper cups of coffee and tea.

Personal & Impersonal Landscapes

for Jim Tate

I. Jim Tate en L'Age d'Or

1930, the
soundtrack, like an old bed
sagging in the middle,
excruciating whine of instruments misrecorded,
collage of fashionable garden parties
with peasants fighting
in the hills — Spanish Civil War —
Dali and Buñuel in Paris
but thinking
of home.
           How
                    you would have loved
the dramatic '30s
when technology was only a rickety structure
over french champagne
and gangsters in pointed-toe shoes.
Even the '60s didn't compare,
though the clothes were more
exciting. I think you wanted the forbidden,
the scandalous/ to claim
the outrageous
as your own. But alas, that is everyone's
fortune now, and no one notices
anything
but anonymous wealth. How dull to make
El Salvador a cause
when history will allow us all to step away
from it, untouched.
We can live in a world of old movies,
infinitely, but should we

69

dance
or fight wars,
other than for fun?

II. Wakoski's Petunias

Ruffled skirts

How we applauded
Sylvia Estrada's flamenco dancing
in Southern California
8th grade.
                  She
was not a Mexican
they said,
            but Spanish/ her father
owned an
orange grove.
Childhood bigotry/ all
we knew,
that some were better than us,
and a few not.
How important those last few,
as we sat on
the sagging screened porch
knowing we had nothing
but our whiteness
and the bank
did not even give credit for that.
I was plump and tired
at 13,
but Sylvia Estrada was a thin hot wire
of brown magnetism. Like a
stick
in her ruffled skirts

and rhythm, thinness, make-up curls,
money
I would never have.

How we applauded.
I still think longingly
of the flamenco clatter and pistol fire
on the old Washington School
Auditorium floor.

Small Things

A smell could drive you away.
His aftershave lotion,
for instance,
sweet as rotting flesh, his elderly chin
never shaved quite smooth, the
grey stubble, like the mold on refrigerator leftovers,
exuding the fragrance
I found so repellent.
                    His wife,
Grandma Vandenbrock,
fat and soggy as boiled cabbage
in clean print housedresses which also
smelled of some
dimestore perfume, Evening in Paris?
a place neither would ever go,
living in their garage apartment next door
to us in La Habra, California,
cooking pot roast on Sunday,
watching Liberace
after church, the smells of the old;
when, I wonder, will they start wafting
from my own body
up to my nose, that awful
aftershave, cleanliness
no help against
rot.

Breakfast at George and Molly Wickes'

The checked cloth,
the muffins,
and the tea. The marmalade
and jams
            in the woodsy edge
of an Oregon town
telling me
morning is a time
I need to get
acquainted with.
I associated it with fatigue,
days I wish did not have to be lived through,
not accomplishment
but endurance.

This, my own attitude
of impatient forebearance,
New England
not in my blood,
the West, dust, the desert of another day.
How I want to rise each morning,
overlook the ocean (to the West)
drink my tea with a view
Balboa might have had.

At your table
morning itself, apart from landscape,
presented fingers and toes,
the cream new with possibilities,
the jams, not death (poison sugar)
but just the right
sweetening for a day. Was John Cage joking
when he said
there's just the right amount

of evil in the world?
If only I could perceive that Truth
and find each morning
new and clear
as Jeffers' view of our Pacific
Ocean.

   *   *   *

And my memory of the peaceful
clear
tree-filled morning
with breakfast at your satisfying
table.

The Tree

outside the north window
has moss growing around its total
circumference. Does this mean
there is only a north? No
south or east or west? How little
I know about trees, even few names,
though flowers have always yielded
information like little pellets falling out of their petals,
to me.

Possessions rigidify a man or woman.
Even the people you love,
making you stiffen yourself
in a discipline against your annoyance
at the way they eat, or blow their noses.
You know
you love them, yet petty
observations irritate you so much you
dare
not think of them. When
no one
is listening, you say,
"I hate (blank)," thinking the forbidden
loved-one's name. Then
you tell yourself how bad you are
and try to think of flowers,
or Mozart, or losing yourself in books about
violent death. Where is Beethoven,
surely a man whose habits would have made any
lover hate him? Bukowski too
has discovered he'd rather live alone, as Pound
discovered he'd prefer
most of the time
not to speak.

The couple in the Nebraska steak restaurant last night,
who sent back their steak,
were embarrassed, but not so much they didn't do it.
No thanks from the waitress.
Adjustment of price
from the management. A tree
with moss growing
on all sides must be a modern
product, like all
of us, not willing to declare boldly
he'll grow his moss on the North side, or
not at all. Usually doesn't send back his steak,
no matter how bad. He covers
as they say,
all the bases. No good
if you're lost and need direction, the moss
on all sides saying they're all
north,
like the love which is no good
if you want romance
or sex instead,
but much better if you want a calm
and peaceful
everyday life, one where you assume
you'll never
be lost in a forest.

Blossoms

look different
when the sun like a hand with sturdy clean
nails
cups
and holds them.
                    Sunset, yesterday,
for instance,
they were used so well
by the light.
            This
                    morning,
a chilly wind gives them
the aspect of
seagulls.
I
almost hear
the foamy surf
whisking under them,
the gulls floating
on this
storming wind,
resting with its drafts,
banking,
tilting,
their voices even seem to sound
outside this window.

I know it's
only
only chickadees
and my back yard nowhere near
the sea.
How I love this warm lamplight,
inside,

the showy bridal white blossoms bobbing
in today's dark spring wind.
The peace of morning
and this moment when I suspend time,
put off the day's chores,
think only of different aspects
of the blossoms
                    (or is it light? Of course,
different
aspects of light.

Gourds

How do you
push winter
off your eyes? The snow on
the ground
that two months ago was a cheek
which grapey gourd and cucumber leaves
nestled fuzzily against.
                            All
this time
the air contained
the possibilities
of snow, just as our bodies always
contain
the possibilities
of sex,
thus we know
that nothing is unexpected,
even when
it is not.

The cucumber, in its somnolent green sheath,
the warty, yellow gourd,
an egg
from a bad marriage,
even the snow which came so early
this year,
and some tips of bitter arugola
poking old leaves out
of its delicate, unexpected crust.

Image Is Narrative

(a meditation on Francisco de Zurbaran's
Still Life: Lemons, Oranges and a Rose)

The lemons are for health and the sourness
of life, unless you understand it.
The tricks in life
are that nothing is hidden, only obscured
by desire, which makes us long
for what we do not have.

The oranges have their zest. Yet,
how pale they are. The
same colour as the lemons, but with them are
leaves and stems and, of course,
some blossoms. Why
are orange blossoms
for weddings?
The lemon blossoms look and smell
the same. How
we choose
to obscure and
misunderstand.

The rose is on a tray next
to a cup of coffee. Why
isn't this painting entitled, "Still Life:
Lemons, Oranges, a Rose, and a Cup
of Coffee"?

Perhaps the cup
is empty
next to the fully bloomed rose? The oranges
take up the most space, even though
they are physically a bit smaller

than the lemons. That is because they are elevated
in a woven wicker basket, like a pedestal;
and the oranges are like an actress
on stage, with a wreath of fragrant star-white blossoms,
despite their pale lemon colour,
and their dainty roundness.
These facts assure me that in Spain
in the early 17th century, one painter, at least,
wanted us to see
that even though he knew all
about it,
he wouldn't give away any of the
real secrets
of marriage.
But in this frozen scene,
this "still life,"
I for one read the empty cup,
the bloomed out rose,
those large lemons — three, as in fates or furies —
and find it not just for the contrast with
the pale yellow fruit
that the whole ground of the painting, including
the surface of the table,
is black.

Black as a night in the garden
when the young bride is wearing her wreath of orange
        blossoms,
having been married to someone she's never met,
who now is drunk and pinching her breasts
like those oranges, those juicy
lemons, the rose from her hair,
fallen to the ground,
and there is only night ahead. Night
to be gotten through, now that the

guests are gone,
and all the cups empty.

I do not need a single human
in the picture
to tell me this story.

In Response to Grey

upon reading Hayden Carruth's excellent
essay about Richard Hugo's *Collected
Poems*, and an angry reply which defended
all of Hugo's weaknesses, without paying
attention to his strengths

In fashion designer windows
and salons of Henry James-ish people,
grey is the colour of elegance.   Always,
grey is offset by slight touches
of cerulean, or aquamarine, or emerald.
And the fabrics shimmer,
reflecting their own internal gleamings of mauve
or silvered blue.
Grey brims with possibility and restraint.
The glorious colours not peacocked
but muted with the control of a smooth glove.

When you
used the word "grey" 12 times in your letter,
not once did it mean "elegant,"
"iridescent," or "shimmering with light." Always,
it meant "drab,"
or "boring,"
or "undistinguished." What a pity your grey eyes
were not those of Minerva,*
but then I've always thought
we expected too much
of our poets;

and that wisdom is a gift which might have
two aspects,
two faces.

---

*The goddess of wisdom, her epithet was "the grey-eyed one."

Lunch with Miriam & Toby

Bielo Polje means
White Field.

Lunch over a meadow of flowers
   the field of white poppies,
   asters of linen,
   a rose with lips of damask,
   white flowers,
   daisies,
in the mountains of Montenegro,
a day of names
     Be-el-a-
 poll-yeh

Miriam, I think of you
with your mouth of petals
saying to me that my memories
of my father
in Max's Kansas City
made you cry.
     20 years ago,
petals,
petals,
fields of white flowers
      I remember
today,
the rainy-day Philadelphia lunch,
artichokes, their big leaves
being scraped into our mouths,
petals,
petals,
I remember you,
think of this web, queen anne's lace,
wild carrot,

the thistle,
chicory on the hillsides,
petals,
petals, artichoke leaves,
fields of white flowers,
to connect our mouths,
our words,
our lives.

What Happened

between 1850 and 1855
when Whitman lost his pretentious sense
of language and somehow got
the voice of an angel?

or between 1905 and 1915
when Stevens suddenly left Edwardian
language and found his belcanto voice?

What happened between 1963 and 1968
when Dorn left his small obscure Creeleyesque lyrics
to find the breadth to write *Gunslinger*?

It's not like flowers where one day you have
a bud, and the next day a flower. It's different,
as if one day you had a messy bag
of rotting garbage and old food, and the next
day it's transformed into fresh strawberries and cream.

What happened?

It is hopeful,
I think.

Saturn's Rings

I don't know if it is a function of middle age, or of being a poet, or some housewifely or scholarly urge, but the desire to order more and more overwhelms me. Thus, in putting together any group of poems, I want to draw from all my poems written over the past twenty-five years. The motif of the ring glints throughout my poetry from the very beginning. It is hard for me to feel that the following small collection is complete without some poems from the past which I do not include for a number of reasons.

Thus, I offer this bit of ordering: "Saturn's Rings" is not complete without my poem "Ringless," which was first published in *Inside the Blood Factory* (Doubleday); my poem "The Ring," from *The Man Who Shook Hands* (Doubleday); my poem "Coins & Coffins," from *Trilogy* (Doubleday); and a poem called "The Dark Procession," from my most recent collection *The Magician's Feastletters* (Black Sparrow). There is also a poem by another poet, Denise Levertov, which I cherish and which to me is oddly part of my own work, "The Wedding Ring," from her collection *Life in the Forest* (New Directions).

The Ring of Irony

What do you say to the mother
of a homosexual man
whom you once were married to,
when she asks you to return your wedding ring
because it's a family heirloom?
    "I want to keep it on my key ring
    where I carry it now,
    to remind me of loss?"
or perhaps, in spite,
    "It was the only thing
    I ever got out of the marriage.
    No. I won't give it back."
Do you say that you love irony
and have imagined your whole life
governed by understatement
and paradox?
Yet, the obvious dominates and
I ask myself,
"Why do you want to keep it?
Surely the woman deserves some comfort/
if a small piece of gold can do it,
who can object?"
Wallowing again, in the obvious,
I wonder at my meanness,
my own petty anger
at men who love other men,
alas, some of them are/have been
my best friends. Irony?
No. The obvious.
Why do you want that circle of gold
lying in your purse with keys
and checkbooks? I nudge myself.
Why don't you purchase an ounce of gold
and carry it in a velvet bag instead. Your

own.
Worth so much more.
Of course. The obvious.
Because the other was given,
not bought, and you
have never asked the return of your gifts, but
you know, Diane, why
you anguish over putting the ring in the box and
mailing it off to
Corona, California.
So obvious.
Because you believe in the gifts
freely given
to appease destiny.
You too would sacrifice
Iphigenia or Isaac
for the cap of darkness,
having given your children
for poetry,
having given your sexuality
for beautiful men,
having relinquished honor
for music.
The circle of gold,
that ring, symbolizes
the pact.
To give it back says the giving was meaningless.
Fate does not honor your bargain,
Ms. Wakoski. Not irony,
the obvious:
you have no husband,
        no house,
        no children,
        no country.
You have no fame,
        fortune,

only remaindered books,
and innocent students who
stab you
with their lack of understanding,
asking, no not ironically,
"Did you give a lot of readings
when you were young?"
Finally, the understatement, the irony, when I say,
"yes," and the past swallows up everything,
leaving the obvious,
and now that handsome woman in California
wants to take the ring.

Soap opera of the middle-aged
mid-Western
schoolteacher?
What do you say when irony deserts you
for the maudlin obvious?
"I am mailing you the ring.
Your claim is greater than mine."

Irony? No, the obvious.

Sleeping in the Ring of Fire

> *to Mel Edelstein who said I must be a*
> *superficial person if I really believed that*
> *suffering could be lessened by material*
> *comforts*

Call me a lily
or fading tuberose begonia. For
it is
better
to wake up in sticky summer
to thermal control,
the air conditioned chamber,
the sweet smelling sheets
which have not been twisted,
worn dingy and limp with sweat,
to be the greenhouse flower
protected from battering heat and cold.
It is
better to live through these nights
at least in harmony
with body heat
when the lover, the husband
deserts you
for another bed.
At least
to wake up
to a fresh fragrant world,
the empty other side of the bed
smooth,
untouched,
my own body only
jangled by feelings, thoughts,
ideas, the stalky
fresh flowers of a new day,
not having drooped, faded,

died, the world cool,
my head clear,
my world protected
from extreme heat and my body not
limp with terrestrial fatigue.

I can sit here cool
in a white gown, having
watered my cucumbers and
tomatoes, and think clearly, sedately,
about the empty bed,
the years of empty beds,
the succession of mornings
alone, and knowing the pain
of woman's failure.

But this air conditioned house
guards me, yes
like the cut flower I am
which couldn't take
the heat of Michigan summer
nights.
I long for some ocean,
the cool shore/ its landscape.
But the salt would kill me.

I cannot totally despair
a failure of sex
or youth
or Helenesque allure.
Technology helps me
accept
the empty bed, acknowledge
complete failure
yet sit here
cool

not in despair
somehow in harmony
with an old body.

For the Girl with Her Face in a Rose

This tapestry which I've never seen —
woven in 1901 —
depicts your wish of self,
disembodied,
the face floating in a giant
florabunda,
the seeker near your rose-enclosed lips,
listening for your voice.
Perhaps this is wisdom.

My own wish cannot be seen in any
weaving
but in the flesh itself
of calla lily,
pale curled flowers with their yellow
pollen-covered fingers
on which no one ever slips
a golden ring.

The wish to be alive
at my own death
which I would want never to come
except as the season's apple, plum,
coriander, pansy,
leek, corn.

I would give up any voice,
even the whisper on these pages
if I would not have to die.
If even
I could age until I fall away from my bones
like the sticky apricots
under late summer's buzzing tree.
Not even the wish

to be young and fresh
and eternally a flower.
Rather, not to die.
Not to suffer pain.
Not to lose my breath.

Letter with the Ring of Truth

Dear Clayton,
　　　　In bushel baskets, the yellow pears
bruise each other's bodies with ripeness.
I imagine the late summer pear
orchards of France
because, like most Americans
I think that beauty originates
in Europe,
and I would rather eat Stilton Cheese
than Wisconsin Blue. We say,
"as American as apple pie,"
and count Johnny Appleseed
among our folk heroes,
yet the most delicious Granny Smith
apples I ever ate
found in the Atlanta farmer's market one winter,
were from France,
bearing little round labels depicting the Eiffel Tower,
cracking like rifle shots when
you bit into them, tart
against the English Stilton
or French boucheron.

Emily, Walt, Wallace, Robinson,
all ate American
and never set foot off this continent
except Jeffers who yielded finally in middle age to his wife's
　　　longing
for Europe.

I chide you, my friend, for exploring
the caves of the Dordogne
rather than meandering on the American continent.
Comparing myself to the fat native

palm trees of Southern California
I say I know
my roots,
my American fathers,
and claim my native speech,
but now as I wander in the early autumn-late summer
farmer's market,
I go hunting for Italian tomatoes,
European cucumbers,
and herbs like basil for making pesto,
herbs like tarragon
which grows in French gardens
and which Americans use without imagination.
I want rosemary for my lamb,
a meat few Americans understand,
and while everyone else is ordering his Thanksgiving turkey,
I put in my order
for a goose.

California's wines
I still claim over burgundies
or the fruits of the Côtes du Rhône,
but I reject bourbon or sour mash
whiskey, preferring Scotch or
Irish, and usually prepare
tortes rather than cobblers or pies
when I entertain.
Where do our roots start?
In what we eat,
or what we read? As a
child I was okay. If
you asked me what my favorite foods were
without hesitation I'd say,
    "corn on the cob"
    "watermelon"
    "ice cream." But now

I can go whole years without consuming
any of them.
And when I dream of eating,
it is of chèvres,
french bread,
Granny Smith apples from the Pyrenees,
extra virgin
olive oil, fresh basil
and garlic with imported pasta.

Walt, Emily, how did you resist
these things, maintain
your truth?

The Pacific pounds
at my white, aging feet. I
listen for the voice which belongs
to this shore
and no other. Why do I hear this
mélange of sound?
Now I am walking in the
Michigan farmer's market,
standing near this bushel basket
of yellow Bartlett Pears, grown right here
in a nearby orchard.
That orchard is heavy with
the hum of bees. No one
here has heard of Poire William
or any other eau de vie, though I'm
told some locals, not the Calvinists because they are
      teetotalers,
prepare a potent homemade brew from the
windfalls, a pear cider. As
yet, I haven't tracked it down,
but I wait, remembering my first trip to Michigan
when an English professor who can actually transplant
      successfully

Michigan wildflowers into his garden
served me
Cherry Bounce,
homemade Michigan liqueur.

What is a native American?
Someone who believes in corn?
The "corn-porn lyric"?
Or one who can reconcile everything
because he has such a big map
in his head?

This meander I write to you, Clayton,
who are from Indiana,
heart of the North American continent.
I post it from Michigan, my residence,
to California, my home.
Your home.
At least we know where we stand
no matter
how deeply
or diversely
our roots extend.

More Light, More Light,

(a letter to a publisher)

Dear Bill,
What do I know about astronomy?
Crazy little bookworm
who read about pyramids holding
golden birds who weighed human hearts for goodness,
and a desert, like her own,
which yielded the first writing, like cactus scars,
who dreamed of light years
as if they were a radiant path she could walk on,
alone; who felt the power of naming things
which had never been seen and might not
exist except through
telescopes and on film.

As a child, the fantasy
of myself as the astronomer or Egyptologist
accompanied my dream of being the concert pianist
or brilliant criminal trial lawyer;
all apart from my own frail vegetable personality,
crisp lettuce which quickly wilts in the heat
or whirling planet life. Or a little
acorn squash which keeps and keeps
in its green shell
but can never be made into much
except a bland accompaniment
to rustic autumn food.
What do I know about the rings
of Saturn
or Saturn itself,
having received my first college "C" at Berkeley
in that profound subject, and having hopelessly pursued,
later, a Harvard-Cal Tech astronomer,

who thought I was a little
like a shooting star,
one of many which might glance
across any nighttime sky?

Yet, I have been the moon
too, her silvery translucence still
glowing in my hair
occasionally.
And I have loved the sun,
though now only have allergic-sensitive skin
to show for it.
The day I mailed off my
wedding ring that I'd carried
so long on my key ring,
to the woman in California who requested it,
I opened an old, mildewing trunk,
and another gold ring
fell through the top layer of
rotting cloth and landed
its little round gold self
on a white wool Greek sweater
that for some reason was intact.

And I thought of myself
then
as the rings of Saturn,
not the planet, mysteriously green,
and throbbing in the solar night,
but rather
those chunks of ice, swirling in orbit,
dead stones, without flicker or
life, who become
transformed,
bathed in opal glow as they move
around their gravitational source;

and seen through light years
they seem like rings, girdling
the planet; they seem to
have as much light
as the whole strip of casinos
in Las Vegas.

The illusion is the same as that
the poet projects.

What do I know about astronomy?

I know that it is the poet's art;
the art of studying light.

Saturn's Rings: As Essay On Territory

Suspended in a gravitational field,
the rocks form a perfect ring.
Never settling
but patterned and constant,
moving, as if in formation,
they are an inspiration
against chaos.

*   *   *

But order
is more than the lack of chaos.

*   *   *

This icy planet
where I have banished myself.
This icy planet,
Saturn,
where I feel at home.

*   *   *

Territory
The search for land of one's own, the right to claim it and own
it, is the story of civilization. And whatever moral arguments
you can make for Native Americans or other early peoples who
did not claim lands do not really contradict the fact that one of
the reasons we hold those people to be primitive or undeveloped
is that they did not claim, build, expand, and sophisticate their
ideas through objects, buildings, and claimed boundaries. At
times, it also seems a spurious argument, for there is recorded
history of tribal territory and wars over encroachment on said
territory. My own belief is that the degree of man's civilization

can be determined by how willing he is to expand his territory and how unwilling he is to let anyone else claim what is his. I can hear you saying, "No wonder we have wars," but I also think that without the desire to claim one's territory, there would be no art, no architecture, no religion, no law, government or society.

* * *

A Fable: The Once Promising Writer
Accepts Middle Age & Failure

My search for land began in the desert. For I knew that few wanted arid, alkaline lands; that I would not have to fight for territory there. My life began in a shack without running water or electricity. I cohabited with snakes and coyotes. We never encroached on each other. I hunted for gold and other precious metals. I slept with one blanket and drank from the cactus. I found a small vein of gold in a large mountain, and soon there were others trying to claim my land.

The beauty of the desert is that there is so little on the surface to sustain life. Yet it holds wealth beneath its surface, the metals breathing as if with enchanted carbon life. I wanted to live in touch with the gold and willingly lived a desert life without family, friends or even music to uncover this ore.

When the Thieves came, I thought it was to admire my gold. Childish, I suppose, or stupid. Foolishly innocent as the Native Americans must have been when the first Europeans came and gave them beads for the little rock called Manhattan. Thus, I shared my gold for a while until I realized the Thieves had come to take it away from me. Then I fought to keep my mine, but like the Indian, I was weak and unsophisticated and outnumbered.

Finally, I left for an undesirable land where there was no gold or uranium, accepted a little gold in exchange for my mine, came to the midwest, tired, with enough to buy a house and get a job as an assayer.

Now I dream of the dramatic desert with its shadowed lilac mountains. I dream of opuntia, ocotillo, and night blooming cereus. I know my desert, my land, is in my head, yet I am angry that others own it physically and that my gold is now theirs.

It is a Christian idea that I cling to, which judges that the less material wealth a man has, the closer he is to heaven. But I want my gold, the territory I think of as mine. How much more blessed to give than to receive, I remind myself. But then I face facts: I didn't give away that territory. I lost it, or it was taken away. Just as today's Native Americans lament the loss of their land to European settlers. It is not just the land, the mine, the territory. That place was where the Spirit resided.

Of course everyone cares about territory, but those of us who are savages don't know how to claim ours. Or to keep it. How to hold what is our own. And its counterpart, of course, how to hold it without robbing others, without plundering or claiming the territory of others. In this fable, I lose because I am weak.

*   *   *

"Once burned,
twice shy."
Each night I dream of Saturn.
I catch on fire and become
one of its rings.
Saturn conserves,
holds,
cannot give
for fear of losing all.

In this fable I lose again
because I do not know how to keep the territory
I claim. I fight but
lose. I do not know how to/ or do not wish to/
fight at length. I flee.
Taking with me an old map,
and an image of even more un-
desirable land.

* * *

The Fable of the Greedy Visitor
and the Ungracious Host

You want to give me gifts
because you know
it is more blessed to give than to receive.
Already
you injure me
because I too know that principle,
and it is I who want to be giving the gifts, who want
that beatitude in my life.

You come into my house, into my kitchen,
and take over. You are going
to give me the gift of
>   Szechewan fish
>   Stir fried pork
>   Indonesian chicken
>   Black bean dip
>   Curried eggplant
and while I love to eat
and have enjoyed many Oriental meals
in your Hawaiian home,
since you have come to live in my house, I wonder
why
you don't see
that you're taking over my kitchen.

That is no gift.
It is theft.
I am no bedraggled housewife with five children, tired of
    putting meals
on the table.
Surely you understand territory./ You try to claim it
    wherever you go.
How is it that it never occurred to you that my kitchen
is my territory,
that to cook fine meals in this kitchen
is one of my gifts,
to myself,
to the world.
How is it that you don't see that you come to my mountains
to mine my gold
and call it your wealth?
How is it you don't understand
my anger?
Am I the "Red Indian," the Native American,
simply occupying some choice land you, European Settler,
    want?
How petty and small of me not to give this gift? My
    territory?
Don't I believe that it is more blessed to give than to
    receive?

Here, take my house.
I will move away.
Why should we fight over the kitchen?
Or any territory?
Like the Navajos whom I feel close to,
accepting the desert
as a rich place, partly
because
no one else wanted it,

I have been guilty of too little education, too little building,
too
little claiming.
Now, if I seem listless or cryptic at your feasts,
White Man,
at least you know the reason.
My spirit is in that territory,
and by claiming it, you
have taken the spirit away.
There cannot be two cooks
in one good kitchen.
Or two owners of one piece of land.
If you don't go away,
I will have to.
I try to convince myself
that riches in the head
are the greatest ones. But the spirit
was there
in the kitchen. How
can I exorcise it?
Lure it out
into new unsettled territory?
Someplace where no one wants to go?
But spirit is not easily beguiled
away from its territory.
Shall I leave it for you
with a curse?

For I must give you the kitchen.
It *is* more blessed to give than receive.
This is the text for my life.
But I do accept
one gift from you:
the lesson of the Native American.

I dream now of travelling to Saturn,
new territory,
to start a new life.
This time
in a place so severe
that surely
no one else
would care to live there?
Where at last
whatever I create
may finally be
brilliantly, inexorably
my own.

Wakoski Visits Saturn

Someone who owns golden retrievers
hands me the clipping,
          "King of Spain
          on visit to U.S."
and I settle into my text in the midwest
but the wind blows kelp
and the wet-dog smell of the beach
is not far away.
The rainy night of brittle hermit crabs
could be another one
where wind and rain blow against
California's windows,
and I am looking out
through the swirled glass
to you, coming in a glistening black slicker.

The you I wait for, is the one
with a wedding ring
glinting on your finger,
one that shows you are married
to me.
But instead there is pipe smoke,
the yeasty smell of stale beer
and rotting apples.

This picture on the clipping
shows the thin un-noble face
of a banker, not
the one who had a rare blood disease
and gave me the entire set of Beethoven's symphonies
          conducted by
Herbert von Karajan on Deutsche Grammophon
when I had no stereo,
but rather a face of the third and fourth

pressing of olive oil. He is
obviously not
my King of Spain
whose flamenco boots tapped rhythms
even in the sand
and walked the rainy beach with his golden shanked dogs
running ahead,
spurting sand, also golden but sodden,
and fanning through the air like
love letters which were crumpled
and thrown away before
even posting.

In this season
there is seldom a clear night,
one where I might see Saturn in the sky twirling its wedding
rings.
It is wet
with the ocean.
With the past.
With the season.
I want to go to Saturn.
I want to sit on a hotel balcony there
and look at the rings spinning
perpetually around the planet,
reminding me of my love for gold,
my need for royalty,
all the missing rings from my
Wanda Landowska fingers.

Something Which

Something which
looks like the mind
comes out
      of the mind/ Step
down
could not work, the natural flow
cannot be
the most precious one. Where does all
this
    lead? To Hell? To Love?
                The Walk
in the Herb Garden, The Visit
to Saturn's Hotels: the feeling we all have
that the world
is flying out of control. Why else
so much interest
in sporting events,
and computers? No readers
for poetry,
only writers. Wanting
the control
nobody else can promise.
It is
a disintegrating time.

Volcanic Ashes Smeared on the Saturn Map

The phone line is as thin as old dried spaghetti.
A word or two
breaks its subtle connecting power.
There are phone conversations I imagine
which are clearer and easier to hear than many
I have had.
For instance, the one reported to me, third-hand,
that you made to our mutual friend, Marian,
saying, "My wife threw me out.
I've been so drunk."

But I picture you standing outside a Filipino bar
in Honolulu,
wearing your aviator glasses
with your hair shaved down to the skull,
ex-marine clothes and the inevitable
zoris, almost drowning
in orchids and sweet sweet plumaria or yellow ginger flowers
—Oh, how did New England come to the tropics? Yr
delicate wife, one gardenia on
yr bush of many, the red rock crab
snowy on yr breath in memory,
and friends like heavy
gold grains of wheat flying off the chaff of daily
encounter.

Why do I imagine this phone call
to a friend in the real snow
of December?
I am thinking of a scene nearly 10 years
ago, in the
Los Angeles airport,
M meeting me in silence,
as he had been silent through phone calls

during my month in the mid-West, his driving me
all the way to Laguna Beach,
taking the luggage out of the car,
carrying it inside as if he were a porter,
then saying, "I have to tell you
that I've moved out, and I'm filing
for a dissolution of the marriage."
(Sic. He didn't say "divorce.")

The emptiness, like the aspirin bottle
in the cupboard with only one tablet left,
his refusal to talk.

I think of you now and pray
that phone call I heard about third-hand
was wrong. That your wife,
beautiful waxy-petalled woman is with you
in the cool heights of Kalai, that the
only dissolution there
is the memory of the Leper Colony,
now a tourist attraction,
on the other side of the mountain.

After Moving the Plants to Saturn

Under my newly emerged gloxinia
I have, in lieu of a plate,
placed a plastic frisbee to catch water.
Last night, when I turned off the living room lights
this saucer glowed, Michelangelo's alabaster.

Lying on the California beach at Diver's Cove this summer,
I had thoughts of murdering frisbee throwers
and players of volleyball.
Zooming over my head,
their guided missiles sent dangerous shadows sliding
over my tan, and I lying there, dreaming of the King of
    Spain,
the beautiful homosexual waiters from Tortilla Flats
(Laguna's best Mexican restaurant)
maniacally throwing impossible frisbee catches to each other,
catching them all, of course,
running, their shiny wet muscles moving like train wheels,
like the sand itself as the tide runs up and back,
the sandpipers on rapid little feet imitating
its motion
up and down the wet packed granules.

Late one afternoon,
walking on the beach,
I found an abandoned frisbee. On it,
in gold,
were the words, M O O N L I G H T   F R I S B E E .
It was pale, a green-white, like some azaleas.
I took it home,
thinking I could set it under one of my potted plants to
    catch moisture.

Now, in a blizzard in the midwest I dream of summer,
the palm trees,
my own body glistening in the sun, like cognac.
Almost with fondness I remember
those beautiful boys playing hated
frisbee games.
I wonder if this Moonlight Frisbee ever sailed through a
        California night,
glowing above the sand
like some white-breasted osprey flying overhead,
someone's ring gleaming like a fish,
the body warm and gold merging
into the night,
wave crests also gleaming like moonlight or snow.

I go to bed now,
turning out my living room lights,
leaving winter's snowstorm outside my windows,
also a moony whiteness,
and see,
glowing under my new-leaved gloxinias,
a saucer of pale light,
maybe a halo for growing things.
I sleep well, years later,
with that California frisbee there
to soften winter's night.

Joyce Carol Oates Plays the Saturn Piano

> for Joyce Carol Oates who, several
> years ago, began to study the piano
> again

I promised myself
that if, by 40, I had won a Pulitzer Prize for Poetry
I would let myself play the piano again.
This was when I was 20,
still pounding on the keyboard,
relentlessly, as if I were chopping down dozens of trees,
and splitting the logs,
making enough firewood for a castle
to be heated throughout an entire Russian winter.

I longed for tea in Samovars,
and to wear sable.
The Snow Queen glinted snow roses, ice violets, tuna-bright
    daggers,
as I spoke with stiff lips.
My fingers were frozen too,
against the brilliance of local pianists
            Abromovitch,
            del Tredici,
            Goodman,
            Ury.
Unlike you,
during the four undergraduate years,
I did not win a Phi Beta Kappa key,
write three novels and marry my sweetheart. I ran across
Dwinelle Plaza barefooted in winter
carrying a wicker birdcage,
I wept in classes, puffed up like a mushroom,
spoke laments
which embarrassed everyone,
and played, played, played,

Beethoven and
Chopin
mostly, trying to substitute music
for sex, for love, for security and kindness.
Unlike you,
I was no combination,
clicking shut like an expensive lock,
of beauty and brains.
I did not have your dark eyes like Godiva chocolates
or your Emily Brontë smile.
I could not even talk,
though most poets' lips move like a swarm of Japanese
        fantailed
goldfish at feeding, pursing for the scattered breadcrumbs.

It was California, but my lips were rigid
with some Northern climate
outside of geography.
My fingers too, though I flexed and flexed
them.
How I hated the rich girls in my classes
who were being
expensively
psychoanalysed (how I needed to tell
my histories),
and who played Bach
sitting decorously, neatly, on the piano bench
like little hair brushes,
while I grimaced and swayed and rocked on the bench
with each cadence, until my practice room
must have seemed like
an exercise cell for some crippled gymnast,
one who had to do all her exercises sitting
in a single position.

The first years of not playing
were empty ones.
Perhaps I was grateful not to own a stereo, have records or
    afford
many concerts.
From Cage and Creeley I learned about silence.
About the "missing"
as part of the object.
And the possibilities I longed for
bred in this silence.
The Ice Queen showed me the beauty of death,
and longing.
The ice needle words which I could emit
from frozen mouth.

Each decade
I would look at my hands,
losing their muscles and flexibility,
until after 20 years
I realized that I could no more return to playing the piano
with any of the skill I'd worked for
than one could go out on a winter day and pick a favorite
    rose
which he had seen bloom months ago
and remembered,
from that summer. Not even the dried hip
would be there.

And I have passed 40 now,
some years ago.
No Pulitzer Prize.
You have had numerous awards with that big one looming
    up
for you now, very soon,
while my name is never even mentioned in connection
with such things.

And I thought I had forgotten all about that young pledge
until I entered your house
and saw the upright piano covered
with music I used to play,
and heard your voice,
flashing like a marlin when it jumps and twists in Caribbean
    waters,
saying, "Yes I am
taking piano lessons again. I practice
two hours every day."

Envy?
No. Past that.
A sense of failure?
Perhaps. For I gave up something
I loved/ to attain something
unknown, and now I have neither.

What do I have?

I wear the rings of Saturn, all
nine of them on my hands,
and when I listen to the keyboard
I hear a music
beyond what anyone can play.

All that wood I chopped
years ago
makes a bright fire,
and when it is dead,
maybe the cinders will begin to move in orbit,
begin whirling,
begin spinning,
around me. I will be Saturn,
and my rings will be

hundreds of pianos, rotating,
revolving around my dried ashy body.

When you play your piano, Joyce,
a chunk of rock might fall into your garden, near the river,
where an old pike nuzzles down near its industrial bottom.
You will say,
"I am playing Saturn's piano,"
and the ring on your long-married, sweetheart, wonderful
     prize-winning
finger will, perhaps, for a moment
glow, as will the rock in your garden,
as a piano always does
when someone with inspired hands throws it into orbit.

Printed July 1986 in Santa Barbara & Ann Arbor for
the Black Sparrow Press by Graham Mackintosh
& Edwards Brothers Inc. Design by Barbara Martin.
This edition is published in paper wrappers;
there are 300 hardcover trade copies; 200 hardcover
copies have been numbered & signed by the author;
& 50 numbered copies with an original holograph poem
have been handbound in boards by Earle Gray & are
signed by the author.

DIANE WAKOSKI was born in Whittier, California in 1937 and educated at U.C., Berkeley. She has published thirteen collections of poems, and many other slim volumes. Her two most recent collections of poems from Black Sparrow were *The Magician's Feastletters* (1982) and *The Collected Greed, Parts 1–13* (1984). The University of Michigan Press published her criticism in *Toward a New Poetry* (1980). She is currently Writer in Residence at Michigan State University.